BANDHAVGARH AT A GLANCE

ATHARAVRAJ YADAV

XpressPublishing
An imprint of Notion Press

XpressPublishing
An imprint of Notion Press

Old No. 38, New No. 6
McNichols Road, Chetpet
Chennai - 600 031

First Published by Notion Press 2019
Copyright © AtharavRaj Yadav 2019
All Rights Reserved.

ISBN 978-1-64678-317-5

DEDICATED TO MY DAD & MOM

Rajnish Yadav

Reeta Yadav

Contents

ONE
BANDHAVGARH

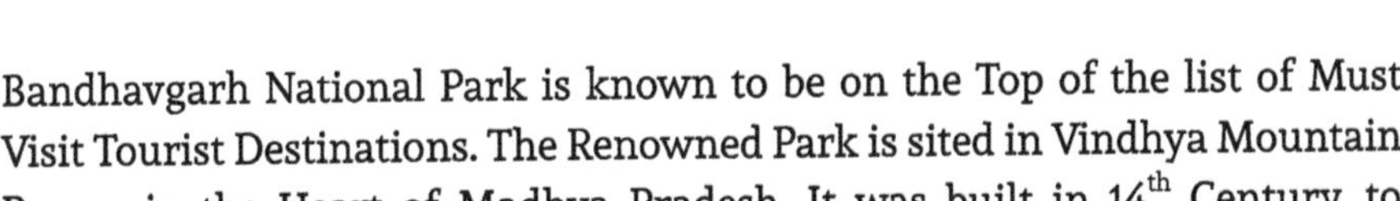

Bandhavgarh National Park is known to be on the Top of the list of Must Visit Tourist Destinations. The Renowned Park is sited in Vindhya Mountain Range, in the Heart of Madhya Pradesh. It was built in 14th Century, to provide a Shelter to Most Rare Animals like Royal Bengal Tigers, Leopards, many Migratory Birds, Cheetals and Countless Fauna.

Bandhavgarh National Park is also known for Keeping the Travelers engaged in the Number of Adventure Activities and Magnificent Places to Visit. One of the Best Activity for Nature Lovers, or Wildlife Photographer, Adventurers is Jungle Safari. Tourists just Enjoy the Thrill of Seeing the Royal Bengal Tiger below them from Elephant Safari or by Jeep Safari. But, One Trip is not Enough for you, to See the Complete Reserve.

So, If You're Planning for a Perfect Trip. We'll Provide you all the Tips, Tricks, Accommodation Hacks, How to Reach, Must Visit Places in or Around Bandhavgarh and many more Information. Let's Explore the Major Tourist Places & Activities, which you should not Miss while touring Bandhavgarh National Park:

Bandhavgarh

Best Zone For Tiger Sighting In Bandhavgarh

While tigers are sighted in almost all the zones of Bandhavgarh, however, Tala zone and Magadhi Zones have better tiger sightings. Tala zone is actually considered as premium zone as owing to more water bodies in Tala zone, the chances of Tiger sighting in summer increases manifold.

Types of Safari

Jeep Safari

Taking a Jeep Safari is One of the Most Astonishing way to Discover and Observe the Flora and Fauna, for all the Travellers. Providing You Broad Opportunity to Spot Rare Species of Wild Animals in their Natural Habitat. Its also a Perfect Option for the Wildlife Photography Enthusiasts.

Charges: – Rs. 5500 per Vehicle (for Indians)

– Rs. 7500 per vehicle (for Foreigners)

Safari Zones: Khitauli Zone, Magadhi Zone, Tala Zone, Bandhavgarh Fort.

Summer Timing : Morning: 5:30 AM to 10:00 AM & Evening: 4:00 PM to 7:00 PM

Winter Timing : Morning: 6:30 AM to 11:00 AM & Evening: 2:30 PM to 5:30 PM

Canter Safari

Canter Safari is the Best Thing to Enjoy the Fun and Adventure in a Single Ride. Canter Safari means taking a Mini Bus to Explore the Glimpses and Landscapes of Bandhavgarh National Park. The Ride is Managed by Madhya Pradesh Tourism Development Corporation. So For Booking the Canter Safari Tickets, You need to Buy Safari Tickets from the Wildlife Department.

Charges: INR 550 per Person per Ride.

Safari Zones: Magadhi, Tala, and Khitauli Zones.

Timings:

Summer: Morning: 5:30 AM to 10:00 AM

Evening: 4:00 PM to 7:00 PM

Winter: Morning: 6:30 AM to 11:00 AM

Evening: 2:30 PM to 5:30 PM

Elephant Safari

Sitting on the Back of an Elephant with a Guide, provides more Thrill into the Journey and a Best Memory in your Complete Trip. It's obvious that the Probability of Spotting a Tiger during Elephant Safari is higher than

spotting during Jeep Safari.
Charges: INR 2800 (Approximately)
Timings:
Morning : 5 AM – 10 AM , Afternoon : 2:30 PM – 5 PM
Duration: 1 to 2 Hours
Safari Zones: Magadhi Zone.

TWO
ACCOMMODATIONS

Samode Safari Lodge

Get an Enhanced Experience by Check-In at the Samode Safari Lodge. The Lodge is encircled by a Serene Landscape of the Jungle. The place provides 12 Independent Mansions, where you get to Spend a Deluxe Vacations and In-House Restaurant and Bar.

Amenities :

• Restaurant

• Bar

• BBQ Facilities

• Swimming Pool

• Fitness Centre

Charges : Rs. 50,000 – 90,000

Location : Mardhari Village, Post Dhamokar, Bandhavgarh

Distance from Bandhavgarh National Park : 30 Kilometres

Tree House Hideaway

Get a Stay at the Magnificent Tree House, encircled by a Beautiful Nature's Landscape. Tree House Hideaway is the Perfect Option of Staying away Hustle Bustle of the City Life.

Amenities :

• Barbeque Grill

• Bar

• Dining Hall

• Restaurant

• Tree House

Charges : Rs. 18,000 – 27,000

Location : Umaria-Bandhavgarh Road, Umaria District

Distance from Bandhavgarh National Park : 500 metres

Aranyak Resort

Aranyak Resort will give you the Feel of Living in a Jungle, by escaping all your Troubles and will Surprise you with Handcrafted Furniture and Countrified Decorations. The Resort is encircled by the Beauty of Nature and the Cottages with all the Modern Features, are a Perfect Place to Enjoy your Holidays.

Amenities :

· Swimming Pool

· Meditation

· Yoga Room

· Amphitheatre

· Restaurant

Charges : Rs. 5,000 – 6,000

Location : Deori Dol, Bijariya Road, Village Kuchwahi, Bandhavgarh

Distance from Bandhavgarh National Park : 2 Kilometers

Kings Lodge

Kings Lodge is the Ultimate Place to Disburse some Time in the Wild, by getting an Amazing View of Forest. Kings Lodge Provides Beautiful Cottages that Features all the Modern Facilities and can be a Memorable Escape from Daily Busy Life.

Amenities :

· Swimming Pool

· Library

· Dining Hall

Charges : Rs. 15,500 – 19,500

Location : Near Tala Gate Bandhavgarh, District Umaria

Distance from Bandhavgarh National Park : 5 Kilometres

Syna Tiger Resort

Syna Tiger Resort is Famed for their Unmatched Lavishness and Seven Theme Based Cottages, with the Mixture of Adventures and Rajasthani Hospitality. Syna Tiger Resort with a Soothing Facilities and a Simple Rural Lifestyle could be a Prominent Escapes from Busy Life.

Amenities :

· Gymnasium

· Swimming Pool

· Bar

· Restaurant

- Café
- Library
    Charges : Rs. 12,000-17,000
Location : Tala, Bandhavgarh National Park
Distance from Bandhavgarh National Park : 500 meters
Mahua Kothi
Mahua Kothi is the Perfect Resorts Domiciled in a Spectacular Panorama, Enhanced by Bamboo & Sal Trees. Mahua Kothi Offers 12 Deluxe Suites that can be Passaged via Private Courtyard.

Mahua Kothi is also infamous for its Diverse Dining Feels like Dining under the Stars and Moonlights with Lanterns and Baghiya Breakfast on a Bullock Cart.

Amenities :
- Spa
- Restaurant
- Garden
- Swimming Pool
Charges : Rs. 21,000-59,000
Location : Bandhavgarh National Park
Distance from Bandhavgarh National Park : 2 Kilometers

THREE
PLACES TO VISIT BANDHAVGARH HILL

In the Reserve, Bandhavgarh Hill is the Highest, in an Altitude of 810 M or Above the Sea Level. There are Many Streams that Emerge from the Hill. The Hill's Plain are encircled by Bamboos and Sal Trees. Bandhavgarh Hill is known for its Cool Climate and Natures Picturesque. The Fascinating View of the Mountains is Visible from, as far as 40 KM.

Baghel Museum

Baghel Museum preserves and showcases the Property of the Maharaja of Rewa. The Museum is a Royal Villa, where the Maharaja's related Property are kept for Showcasing. One of the Most Outstanding Fascination is the Stuffed Boy of the First White Tiger, named as "Mohan", in the Museum.
Timing: January to December: 10:00 AM to 03:00 PM & 05:00 PM to 08:00 PM (All Days Open)
Distance from Bandhavgarh National Park: 120 meters

Bandhavgarh Fort

Bandhavgarh Fort is also known as Bandhavdisha, (Lord of the Forts). The Fort is supposed to be the Construction of around 2000 Years Back. Bandhavgarh Fort is Famous because of a very Popular Legend attached to it. It is Trusted that The Hero of Ramayana, Shri RamJi stayed her for a while after Demolishing the Great Demon, Ravana. Then, Shri RamJi handed over the Fort to his Brother Shri Lakshmana, to keep an Eye on the Side of Lanka.
Timing: 6 AM to 6 PM
Distance from Bandhavgarh National Park: It's in the Park.

Ghorademon Waterfalls

The Waterfall is a Deep and Natural Flowing Rapid, within the Bandhavgarh National Park. The Place creates an Ambience of Peace and Serenity by the Flowing Sound of the Rapids and the Music of the Jungle. Ghorademon Waterfall is a Must Visit Site to get a Vibe of Adventures and Relaxation, being away from Daily Busy Schedules.

Bandhavgarh Caves

Bandhavgarh consists of 40 Caves across the Park Borders. Some Caves covers a length of around 6 KM. Before Walking into these Caves, Seek an Advice from the Local Experts or Guides, coz These could be Dangerous for You, as These Caves became a Shelters for Bears, Tigers, Snakes and many more. One of the Major Cave is known as "Badi Gufa",(Biggest Cave) and is believed to be from 10th Century, by the Locals.

Distance from Bandhavgarh National Park: It's in the Park.

Tala Village

Take a Shelter into the Rural Lifestyle by tripping Tala Village. It's a great Hideout to get the Vibes of Village Life, being away from the Busy City Life. Mud Houses provides the Perfect Blend of Simple Lifestyle. Many Resorts are sited near to this Village.
Timing: Sunrise to Sunset
Distance from Bandhavgarh National Park: It's in the Park.

Bamera Dam

Bamera Dam is a Paradise for Bird Sightseeing and You can Capture countless Rare and Exotic Species of Birds, resting on the Banks of this Dam. Bamera Dam is sited within the Panpatha Sanctuary and is 12 KM Away from Bandhavgarh National Park. This Place could be an Ideal Place for Family Picnic and Enjoy the Serene View of Nature and the Fascination of the Majestic Dam.

Shesh Shaiya

The Statue of Lord Vishnu of around 66 Ft Tall is in a Sleeping Posture on the Shesh Naag (Seven Serpents), is found in Shesh Shaiya. The Statue of Lord VishnuJi is of Primeval, sited near a Green Pool, whose Water is Trusted to be Divine, by the Locals. It is also Trusted to be the Spot, where River Charanganga originated.

Shesh Shaiya is sited on the Bandhavgarh Hill. It is the Single Place in Bandhavgarh, where You're allowed to Go on Foots.

Distance from Bandhavgarh National Park: It's in the Park.

Climber's Point

Climber's Point is a Scenic Viewpoint in the Bandhavgarh National Park. This place is loved by the Adventures, which provides the Picturesque View of the Entire Park, as it is sited at an Altitude of 13,020 Ft above the Sea Level.

JwalaMukhi Temple

Sited around 8 KM from the National Park, on the Shores of River Charanganga. The Temple is Devoted to the Goddess Jwalamukhi. According to the Local Faith, If you Visit the Temple to Worship with Trust and Belief in your Heart & Asks for a Wish, It will Come True. It's a Place to Relax and get a Peaceful Vibes.
Distance from Bandhavgarh National Park: 8 kilometres

FOUR
BEST TIME TO VISIT

Bandhavgarh National Park is Open from the Months of October to June. In Winter Season, from November – March is the Perfect Time to Visit. Monsoon Season is also the Best Season to witness the Lush Green Panoramas at Bandhavgarh National Park. And for Wildlife Photographers, the Months of April, May & June are the Ideal to Visit the Park and Get the Perfect Shot.

FIVE

HOW TO REACH

By Air : Jabalpur & Khajuraho are the Closest Airports.

By Road : Bandhavgarh is well connected with Many Cities like Umaria (30 km.), Katni (105 km.), Satna (160km.), Jabalpur (210 km.), Khajuraho (240 km.) and Many More.

By Trains : The Nearest Railway Stations are of Umaria (30 Km.) and Katni (105 Km.).

The End

Thank You

Ingram Content Group UK Ltd.
Milton Keynes UK
UKHW010606040623
422833UK00002B/221